Operations
in
English

55 Natural and Logical Sequences
for Language Acquisition

Supplementary Materials Handbook Two

Gayle Nelson & Thomas Winters

with illustrations by T. D. Whistler
and A. Mario Fantini

PRO LINGUA ASSOCIATES

Publishers

Published by Pro Lingua Associates
15 Elm Street
Brattleboro, Vermont 05301 USA

SAN 216-0579

802-257-7779
800-366-4775

At Pro Lingua,
*our objective is to foster
an approach to learning and teaching that
we call* **Interplay,** *the **inter**action of language
learners and teachers with their materials,
with the language and the culture, and
with each other in active, creative,
and productive* **play.**

ISBN 0-86647-074-3

This book was set in Electra by Stevens Graphics of Brattleboro, Vermont, and printed and bound by Braun-Brumfield in Ann Arbor, Michigan.

Designed by Arthur A. Burrows after the Newbury House original.

Printed in the United States of America

Publishers' Foreword

Pro Lingua Associates is pleased to publish this thoroughly revised edition of Gayle Nelson and Thomas Winters' original book *ESL Operations*, formerly published in 1980 by Newbury House. When we learned that it was going out of print, we jumped at the chance to add it to our list, quite simply because the basic premise behind the operations, and the easy-to-follow, practical presentation of the procedures make as much sense today as they did thirteen years ago.

This edition, in our opinion, builds on the fundamental strength of the first title and at the same time represents a significant updating and revision. Thirty-two of the original 41 operations have been retained but revised. Some have been dropped (sending a telegram) and some new ones added (sending a fax) to keep up with the times, and overall this edition has been expanded to 55 operations.

One of the significant features of these operations is that they are quite compatible with a wide variety of language teaching approaches. Gayle and Thomas, who have used operations in a variety of settings, had this to say: "*Operations have been and can be used with audio-lingual materials, notional/functional/communicative materials, and the Silent Way. We believe that operations are particularly compatible with Total Physical Response, a method of teaching foreign languages developed by James Asher in which students learn the target language by first listening and responding to the spoken requests of their teachers. Later, students produce the target language in making requests of their fellow students, that is, giving them commands. Similarly, in performing operations, students listen and respond physically to directions given by their classmates.*"

We would also like to point out that operations have definite possibilities for those teachers who are interested in the Natural Approach.

The operations in this book can also be used in and adapted to a variety of teaching contexts. All of them can be done in a classroom, but there are many suggested follow-up activities that can be done as homework or "in the real world" as experiential activities.

Although these operations are especially effective at the beginning and low intermediate proficiency levels, several of them can easily be used at higher levels. A quick glance at the contents will also show that they can be effective with children or adults, and many of the operations grouped under **Classroom Activities, Games and Exercises,** and **Food and Recipes** can be used effectively with very young children.

Finally, we would like to point out one editorial decision regarding the use of the third person singular pronouns. We have decided to use *she, her, hers* as the generic third person forms. *He or she* is unnecessarily clumsy; *he, him, his* have had their chance for several hundred years; and *she* at least includes *he*.

Acknowledgements

We wish to express our thanks to the students and staff of the School for International Training for their suggestions and support and to **Mary Clark** and **Pat Byrd** for helping us with the grammar components in each operation. A special debt of gratitude goes to **Ray Clark** for initiating this project, for continuing to believe in it over the years, for providing helpful ideas, for writing a new operation, "Sending a Fax," and for editing this edition. This book would not exist if it weren't for Ray.

In this new edition, we had contributions from a number of graduate students at Georgia State University. Specifically, we would like to acknowledge **Ron Summer** for "Using a Calculator," **Rebecca Dinkins** for "Learning a New Word," **Harold Rowland** for "Making an Origami Cicada," **Jeff Boddy** for "Having Fun with Poetry," **Jarris Anderson** for "Chewing Gum," **Lauren Gold** for "Making Popcorn," **Tony Dickenson** for "Using a Fast Food Restaurant Drive-Through," and **Donna Worley** for "Using an Umbrella."

Finally, we want to thank the folks at Pro Lingua, a publishing company run by and for language teachers.

Gayle Nelson
Thomas Winters

Contents

Operations

in

English

What Is an Operation?

An operation is a procedure for doing something, using a natural sequence of events. It may involve manipulating a piece of equipment, such as operating a tape recorder; it may relate to skill development, such as using a dictionary; or it may involve body movement, such as touching your toes. The procedure can be as simple as making a cup of instant coffee or as complex as making origami.

The use of language is the essential factor leading the student through the process of correctly completing the operation. In other words, Student A gives directions to Student B, and unless those directions are correct, Student B will not successfully complete the operation. For example, in operation number 44, Mailing a Letter, Student A must instruct Student B to fold the letter before Student B can put the letter in the envelope. Language, therefore, is the medium that enables the student to complete the process, and the process is a vehicle for learning the language. The meaning of the language is made clear by the action, and the action reinforces the language. The experience, therefore, establishes a basis for tactile and visual memory as well as linguistic memory.

An operation is usually a set of instructions delivered in the form of commands. The most useful format is called the 8 by 8, a series of eight commands, each command not exceeding eight words. Students are better able to remember and work with sentences of eight or fewer words. If an operation is much longer, they have more difficulty remembering the steps. In some more complex operations, lines do exceed the eight-word limit. These operations would be used in a more advanced English class, where students would be able to handle longer sentences.

Why Use Operations?

Operations are an effective way for students to use the language actively in a purposeful, functional manner. Since students are physically responding to the words, the language has concrete meaning. As Student A reads the operation to Student B, Student B must focus on the message because she is forced to show whether she has understood. Students demonstrate their understanding by doing the actions.

1

Operations can be used very successfully for teaching and practicing verb tenses. The verbs used in such operations are characteristically high-frequency action verbs, often irregular—*put, hold, open, close, take, give,* and *let*—and phrasal verbs, such as *turn on, pick up, fill in,* and *stand up.* Depending on the level of the class, the teacher may vary the verb phrase by using different verb tenses. For example, if the class were working on the past tense, the question *What did you do?* might be asked at the completion of the operation, thus causing the student to change the verbs to the past form.

Operations can be designed around students' specific needs, for example, Using a Dictionary (7) or Using a Pay Telephone (45), thereby increasing their motivation and retention. They can also be used for cross-cultural situations, such as Using a Fast Food Restaurant Drive-Through (43) or Writing a Check (49). Operations can develop into dialogue sequences. For instance, in the operation Having Fun with Poetry (16), students spontaneously ask and answer questions about the poem they have chosen. After reading a short poem, a student may ask what someone liked or didn't like about it, what the poem was about, or what the poem reminded her of.

Operations add variety to the class, and students enjoy doing them. The teacher withdraws from direct participation early in the lesson; therefore, **the students are able to perform and practice by themselves.** Because operations are short, they can easily be covered in a class period.

When to Use Operations

Operations should be used as a supplement to the regular curriculum. For example, after working with irregular past forms, the teacher may select an operation, such as Lighting a Candle (17), that uses several irregular verbs. After the student has completed the operation, the teacher asks, "*What did you do?*" eliciting the response, "*I **lit** the match and then **held** the flame next to the candle wick.*"

Operations can be used at any level of English proficiency, although they work best at beginning and intermediate levels. An operation on Eating a Cookie (33) works well in a beginning class because the students have an opportunity to use verbs they know such as *open, close, take,* and *give.* For beginning classes, the operations are purposely short. Advanced classes may also use operations; for example, the operation on

Filling in a Form (52) may be used in a class that is preparing for university study in the United States.

Operations can be used as supplementary activities when working on verb tenses, intonation and stress patterns, vocabulary building, cultural information, word order, possessive forms, locative and directional phrases, questions, or adverbs. They are recyclable in that the teacher may use a specific operation once and then return to it a few weeks later, changing the point of emphasis. For example, the focus may be a specific verb tense in the initial presentation and intonation patterns in the second presentation.

How to Use Operations

Operations can be used in a variety of ways and as a supplement to a variety of methods. Three possible presentations are given here; the second two are variations of the first. Each class and teacher should, however, develop their own way of using operations. These examples are simply suggestions to help a class that is beginning to use operations.

Example 1

The teacher is responsible for setting up the environment and bringing in necessary materials. The teacher should have the operation memorized. In the initial presentation, the teacher introduces the piece of equipment or materials to be used, pointing out the parts and introducing unfamiliar vocabulary. The teacher then models the sequences of actions, demonstrating the use of a piece of equipment, making something, or doing some action. For example, in the operation on Mailing a Letter (44) the teacher says, *"Fold the letter to fit the envelope"* and then completes the action by folding the letter to fit the envelope. The teacher says each line of the operation and then performs the action until the operation is completed. The students then open their textbooks. The teacher may lead the class through a choral repetition, listening for stress patterns, pronunciation, and intonation.

Two students now perform the operation, modeling it for the rest of the class. For example:

Student A: *Fold the letter to fit the envelope.*
Student B: (folds the letter to fit the envelope)
Student A: *Put the letter in the envelope.*
Student B: (puts the letter in the envelope)

The student giving directions has her book open, and the student receiving directions has her book closed. After completing the operation once, the students switch roles and perform the operation again. The class observes the two students.

Next, all the students practice the operation in pairs, each student taking a turn at giving and receiving directions. Students giving directions have their books open and read the operation. Students receiving directions have their books closed and perform the actions.

If the class were working on a particular grammar point, a question-response sequence might be used after the completion of each step to provide practice in that particular point. For example, if the class were studying locative phrases, the question-response sequence might go as follows:

> Student A: *Put the plate in the center of the placemat.*
> Student B: (puts the plate in the center of the placemat)
> Student A: *Where is the plate?*
> Student B: *It's in the center of the placemat.*
> Student A: *Put the napkin to the left of the plate.*
> Student B: (puts the napkin to the left of the plate)
> Student A: *Where did you put the napkin?*
> Student B: *I put it to the left of the plate.*

Finally, the students again perform the operation, but with their books closed. They may vary the words, as long as the meaning is retained and the sentences are grammatically correct.

In summary, the first presentation is as follows:

A. Introduction
  1. The teacher introduces the materials and new vocabulary.
  2. The teacher gives the directions and performs the sequence of actions.
  3. The students open their textbooks.
  4. The teacher may choose to lead the class through a choral repetition.
  5. Two students model the complete operation.

B. Class practice
  1. The class divides into pairs and performs the operation.
  2. The students perfom the operation with their books closed.

Example 2

The students read the operation silently to themselves. After they finish, the teacher asks if they have any questions regarding pronunciation, vocabulary, grammar, or overall comprehension. After the questions have been answered, two students or the teacher and a student perform the operation, one giving directions and the other responding. The class then divides into pairs and performs the operation. For example:

> Student A: *Take a book.*
> Student B: (takes a book)
> Student A: *Open it to the first page.*
> Student B: (opens it to the first page)

The students giving directions have their books open, and the students receiving directions have their books shut. After the operation is completed, the students change roles and do it again.

After everyone has completed both roles in the operation, the students close their books and again perform the operation as well as they are able. The students may vary the words, as long as the meaning is retained and the sentences are grammatically correct.

In summary, the second presentation is as follows:

A. Introduction
1. Students read the operation.
2. Students ask questions.
3. Two students or the teacher and a student may perform the operation.

B. Class practice
1. The class divides into pairs and performs the operation.
2. The students again perform the operation, but with books closed.

Example 3

Really a variation of the first two types, this presentation can be used after students are familiar with the pair procedure. The advantage of this variation is that the task of figuring out the operation is given to the students. The teacher acts as a resource person who answers specific individual questions. In this variation, the class divides into pairs, and the teacher assigns the operation. The teacher should select an operation that the students will be able to do on their own. The teacher is also responsible for each pair having the necessary materials. The students then perform the operation. Student A begins with her book open and reads the operations to Student B. Student B has her book closed and follows the directions. When Student B has finished the last step of the operation, they switch roles. Student A closes the book and Student B opens the book and reads the operation to Student A. After both students have performed both roles, they both close their books. Again, Student A gives directions to Student B. When finished, Student B gives directions to Student A. They may vary the words as long as the meaning is retained and the sentences are grammatically correct.

In summary, this third variation is as follows:

A. First performance
>   1. Student A has the book open and reads the operation to Student B.
>   2. Student B has the book closed and follows Student A's directions.

B. Second performance
>   1. Student B has the book open and reads the operation to Student A.

C. Third and fourth performances
>   1. Both students close their books. Student A gives the directions. Student B follows the directions and performs the operation.
>   2. Student B gives the directions and Student A follows them.

A *Sample Operation in Full*

To further clarify the pair interaction between students and suggest two ways of building on an operation, here is an example using Drawing a Picture (1). Student A has her book open. Student B has her book closed. Student A reads the operation from the book, one step at a time, and Student B responds.

> Student A: *Draw a lake.*
> Student B: (draws a lake)
> Student A: *Draw two trees next to the lake.*
> Student B: (draws two trees next to the lake)
> Student A: *Draw a rock between the trees.*
> Student B: (draws a rock between the trees)
> Student A: *Draw a fish in the lake.*

6

Student B: (draws a fish in the lake)
Student A: *Draw the sun over the lake.*
Student B: (draws the sun over the lake)
Student A: *Draw two birds near the trees.*
Student B: (draws two birds near the trees)
Student A: *Draw grass around the lake.*
Student B: (draws grass around the lake)

After Student B has finished, Student A asks, *"What did you do?"* Student B tells what was done in her own words. For example:

> *I drew a lake on the paper. Then I drew two trees near the lake and put a rock between the trees. Next, I drew a fish in the lake and the sun over the lake. I also drew two birds near the trees and put some grass around the lake.*

Now Student B opens her book and gives directions to Student A. Student A closes her book and follows the directions.

After both students have completed the operation, the teacher asks them to write a paragraph titled "Drawing a Picture." In the paragraph, they are to use transition words, such as *first, second, next, then, after that,* and *finally.*

The effectiveness of an operation lies in the interaction between the students working in pairs—the speaking, the listening, the understanding, and the doing.

Seven More Variations

Here are some additional ideas for presenting and using operations.

Variation 1. Students write their own operations, bring in necessary materials, and perform them in class.

Variation 2. Students write each step of an operation on an index card, mix up the steps, and then give them to another student, who puts them in the correct order and performs the operation.

Variation 3. Students illustrate each step of an operation on separate index cards, and then give them to another student, who puts them in the correct order and writes an operation or paragraph to match the illustrations.

Variation 4. Students mime an operation while other students watch, guess the activity, and then explain it orally.

Variation 5. In order to give students additional practice in spoken English, add appropriate words or phrases to the commands, thus providing transitions or creating polite requests. For example, the operation Using a Dictionary (7) can be modified in the following manner:

> **First,** *look at the first letter of the word.*
> **Please** *open the dictionary.*
> **Next** *find the section with words starting with that letter.*
> *Look at the second letter of the word,* **please.**
> **Now** *find the words starting with those two letters.*
> **Next you** *look at the words at the top of the page in the dictionary.*
> **OK, now** *notice if your word falls between them.*
> **Finally, you're ready to** *find the word and read the definition.*

Other ways of introducing commands include:

> *Would (Will) you please . . .*
> *At this point, you should . . .*
> *Now try to . . .*
> *Next you can . . .*
> *You will (can, may, should) now . . .*
> *Would you mind _____ ing . . .*

Variation 6. Operations also provide excellent practice in asking questions. If the class is learning or practicing a specific verb tense, the following chart provides examples of the kinds of questions that may be used.

Verb Tense	Sample Questions
Present continuous	*What are you doing?*
Past	*What did you do?*
Future	*What will you do? What are you going to do?*
Present perfect	*What have you just done?*
Past continuous	*What were you doing a minute ago?*
Future continuous	*What will you be doing next?*

8

Students can write and/or ask other kinds of questions, including **yes-no** questions and **WH** questions. Some questions are:

Did he put coffee into her cup?
Should I write down the telephone number?
Who lit the match?
How are you pouring the water?
Where does the fork go?
Why do you write checks?

Students can write and/or ask questions before, during, or after an operation.

Variation 7. Finally, many of the operations in this book can be expanded into dialogue sequences with both Student A and B asking questions, giving commands, and responding with both words and actions. In fact, five of the operations in this book are presented in dialogue sequence forms, one in each of the first five sections. They are operations 9, 25, 32, 42, and 48.

As an example, two students (or the teacher) could take the operation Setting a Table (18) and rewrite it into the following dialogue.

Original Operation (18)

1. Put the plate in the center of the placemat.
2. Fold the napkin.
3. Put the napkin to the left of the plate.
4. Place the knife to the right of the plate.
5. Put the teaspoon to the right of the knife.

Dialogue Sequence

Student A: Where do I put the plate?
Student B: Put it in the center of the placemat, and then fold the napkin and put it to the left of the plate.
Student A: (puts the plate and napkin on the placemat)
Student B: Now I have the silverware. Where does it go?
Student A: First put the knife to the right of the plate and then the spoon to the right of it.
Student B: (places the knife and spoon) OK?
Student A: Yup. OK, now put the fork . . .

9

Two students who did not write it are given the written dialogue. After practicing it, they perform it without notes. This is quite effective if pairs of students exchange original dialogues and perform them for each other. The performer can make corrections and changes, but should discuss any changes with the author pair after the performance.

How to Use This Book

The operations in this book are divided into six categories. Within each category, the operations are sequenced in order of difficulty, so that the later operations require a higher level of vocabulary and a greater knowledge of grammatical structures than do the earlier ones. Operations were selected on the basis of their accessibility and adaptability. Therefore, most of the operations in this book make use of simple materials or materials that are easily obtainable and can be used in the classroom. A few of the operations use materials that are often inaccessible, but these operations can be mimed, for example, Using a Vending Machine (51).

The format is the same for each operation. The title is given first, followed by the materials needed to perform the operation. Key words that occur in the operation are listed, with the verbs listed as infinitives. Next comes the operation itself, broken down into steps. After the operation, grammar notes are presented, including the structures that occur repeatedly in the operation or that are likely to cause students difficulty. The grammar notes are mainly for the use of teachers. The final section gives follow-up activities that relate to the operation. Students should have performed the operation at least once before they do the follow-up activities. The follow-up section includes activities that are more creative, such as writing an original operation or a story. Questions that are given can be assigned as homework or done in class. The section also gives ideas for discussion, connected discourse, and games.

Use this book as a guide. You do not need to use all the operations or use them in the given sequence. These operations should be adapted to meet the specific needs of your class.

CLASSROOM ACTIVITIES

1. Drawing a Picture

Materials   paper, pencils

Key words

grass	a fish	next to	around
a lake	a bird	in	near
a tree	the sun	between	
a rock	to draw	over	

Operation

1. Draw a lake.
2. Draw two trees next to the lake.
3. Draw a rock between the trees.
4. Draw a fish in the lake.
5. Draw the sun over the lake.
6. Draw two birds near the trees.
7. Draw grass around the lake.

Grammar notes

locative phrases — *next to*
count and noncount nouns — *two trees, grass*
definite and indefinite articles — *a lake, the sun*

Follow-up

1. Student A dictates the operation to Student B. Student B writes down what Student A says. After you're finished, check your work with your text. Change roles, so Student A becomes Student B, and do it again.

2. Write an operation on drawing a house, an article of clothing, or a face.

2. Coloring the Picture

Materials   the picture from the operation Drawing a Picture (1), colored pens, pencils, or crayons

Key words

a frog	blue	green
to color	brown	yellow
do not		

Operation

1. Color the lake blue.
2. Color the trees green and brown.
3. Draw a frog on the rock.
4. Color the frog green.
5. Do not color the fish.
6. Color the sun yellow.
7. Do not color the birds.
8. Color the grass green.

Grammar notes

shift from *a* to *the*
negative imperative form: ***do not** color*

Follow-up

1. Do the operation again and substitute other colors. For example: *Color the frog red. Color the sun purple.*

2. Experiment with your vocabulary. Write an operation for drawing and coloring a picture. Then read your operation to another student, and she will follow your directions. Continue until the picture is finished. Change roles.

3. Practice using the contraction *don't*.

3. Playing with Numbers

Materials   paper, pencils

Key words

a sum	to subtract	to add
a total	to multiply	to write down
to remember	to divide	in your head

Operation

1. In your head, add 5 and 7 and 3.
2. Remember the sum.
3. Subtract 5 from the sum.
4. Multiply by 7.
5. Divide by 2.
6. Add 5 to the total.
7. Write down the number.

Grammar notes

verb-preposition combinations — *subtract **from**, multiply **by***

Follow-up

1. After each step, Student A ask a *yes/no* question. For example: *Did you add 5, 7, and 3?* Student B answers the question.

2. Student A gives Student B a more complicated mathematical problem. For example, Student A says, *Add 116 and 279. Now subtract 189 from the total.* Continue giving directions until the problem is completed. Change roles.

3. Write an operation on averaging numbers.

4. Using a Calculator

Materials   several calculators

Key words

a calculator	an addition sign	to press	to take
a button	a multiplication sign	to turn on	to say
an equals sign	a division sign	to turn off	to clear

Operation

1. Take a calculator.
2. Press the red button to turn it on.
3. Press nine, the addition sign, eight, and the equals sign.
4. Press the subtraction sign, nine, and the equals sign.
5. Press eight, the multiplication sign, and the equals sign.
6. Say the answer.
7. Press the red button to clear the answer.
8. Turn the calculator off.

Grammar notes

phrasal verbs—*turn on, turn off*
nouns in a series
compound nouns—addition *sign, subtraction sign*
infinitive phrase (adverbial)— *to turn it on*

Follow-up

1. Student A gives Student B a more complicated problem. For example: Student A says, *Press the number 1,987. Now press the multiplication sign and then press 304. What is your answer? OK, now press the division sign and number 9. What is your answer?* Continue giving directions until the problem is completed. Change roles.

2. Introduce the words *plus, minus, times,* and *divided by.* Student A asks B questions such as, *What is 48 plus 65? What is 107 minus 56?* and B figures out the answers on the calculator. Change roles.

5. Using a Blackboard

Materials   a blackboard, chalk, an eraser

Key words

chalk	an eraser	to erase	to put
a blackboard	to pick up	to stop	near
a tray	to hold		

Operation

1. Pick up a piece of chalk.
2. Hold it near the blackboard.
3. Write your name on the blackboard.
4. Stop writing.
5. Put the chalk in the chalk tray.
6. Pick up the eraser.
7. Hold it near the blackboard.
8. Erase the blackboard.

Grammar notes

locative phrases — *near the blackboard*
compound nouns — *blackboard, chalk tray*

Follow-up

1. Do it again with more instructions for step 3. For example:
   Student A gives directions to Student B for drawing a picture.
   Student A: *Draw a clown.*
   Student B: (draws a clown)
   Student A: *Draw a duck on top of the clown's head.*
   Continue until the picture is completed. Then change roles.

2. Rewrite the operation, adding descriptive adjectives to each step.

6. Giving Classroom Instructions

Materials whatever is found in the classroom

Key words

a thermostat	to turn on	to turn up	to put away
a shade	to turn off	to turn down	to open
to pull	to lock	to take out	to close

Operation
1. Open/close the door.
2. Lock/unlock the door.
3. Turn on/turn off the lights.
4. Turn up/turn down the thermostat.
5. Open/close a window.
6. Pull up/pull down a shade.
7. Write on/erase the blackboard.
8. Take out/put away your textbook.

Grammar notes

phrasal verbs — *turn on, turn off*

Follow-up
1. Give as many directions as you can think of. For example: *jump, hop on one foot.*
2. Do the operation again. This time Student A adds an adverb of manner, for example, *quickly,* to each step when giving directions to Student B. When Student A is finished, Student B adds adverbs of manner while giving the directions to Student A.
3. In three minutes, write down as many things in the classroom as you can. The person with the highest number of objects written down is the winner.

4. In five minutes write down as many commands as you can. The commands must include items in the classroom. A verb can only be used once. The person with the highest number of objects written down is the winner.

5. Develop a set of instructions with affirmative and negative commands like these: *write, print, repeat, listen, spell, define, translate, tell, say, speak, imitate, whisper, copy.* Also see Operation 29, Would You Please.

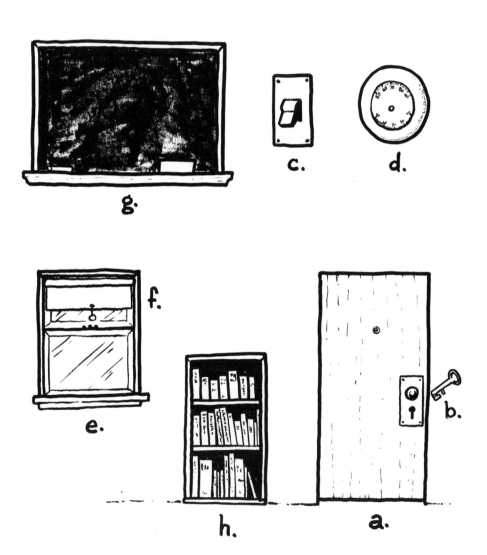

7. Using a Dictionary

Materials   a dictionary, a word to be looked up

Key words

a letter	the top	to fall between	to notice
a dictionary	a definition	to find	to read
a section	to look at	to open	first
			second

Operation

1. Look at the first letter of the word.
2. Open the dictionary.
3. Find the section with words starting with that letter.
4. Look at the second letter of the word.
5. Find the words starting with those two letters.
6. Look at the words at the top of the page in the dictionary.
7. Notice if your word falls between them.
8. Find the word and read the definition.

Grammar notes

-*ing* phrases used as noun modifiers — *words **starting with***
ordinal numbers — *first, second*
if clause

Follow-up

1. Do the operation again and add phrases that make the steps polite. For example: ***Please** look at the first letter of the word. **Now would you please** open the dictionary. . . . .*

2. List and describe the various sections of the dictionary.

3. Rewrite the operation as a paragraph. Use the past tense, and combine some of the sentences.

8. Learning a New Word

Materials dictionaries, index cards, pencils or pens

Key words

a dictionary	one side	to take	to write	funny
an index card	the other side	to open	to say	quickly
		to find		

Operation

1. Take a dictionary.
2. Open it to any page.
3. Find a word that you don't know.
4. Take an index card.
5. Write the word on one side of the card.
6. Write the definition of the word on the other side.
7. Write a funny sentence with the word.
8. Say the sentence three times quickly.

Grammar notes

locative phrase — *on one side*
adjective clause with *that*
shift from *an* and *a* to *the*
of phrase showing possession
adverbs of frequency and manner

Follow-up

1. Perform the operation together as a team. One student completes steps 1 to 5, and the other completes steps 6 to 8. Then tell the teacher what you did.

2. Trade index cards with each other and complete steps 6, 7, and 8.

9. Practicing Politeness

Materials   a book or other small object

Key words

excuse me	please	thank you	to apologize
sure	would you mind	sorry	to wait
OK	not at all	that's OK	to take

Operation: Dialogue Sequence

Student A: *Excuse me.*

Student B: *Sure. What do you want?*

Student A: *Please take my book for me.*

Student B: OK. (Takes the book.)

Student A: *Would you mind taking it to the window and holding it for me?*

Student B: *Not at all.* (Takes the book to the window.)

Student A: *Thank you. I have an errand to do. I'll be back in a minute.* (A leaves the room for a few moments and then returns.)

Student A: *Sorry I'm late. How long have you been waiting?*

Student B: *About five minutes.*

Student A: *Oh dear. I do apologize.*

Student B: *That's OK. Here's your book.* (B returns the book to A.)

Grammar notes

would you mind + gerund
How long question
do for emphasis

Follow-up

1. With the teacher, your class can write a number of polite phrases on the blackboard. Then vary this operation, using the additional forms of politeness and instructing each other to do as many activities as you can think of. For example: *I hate to bother you, but would you mind lending me a pencil?*

2. Listen to native speakers of English talking and write down any words or phrases that indicate politeness. In class, combine your lists. For additional follow-up, discuss who used these polite expressions in what situations. For example, was the expression *Pardon me* used by a woman or a man? Was the expression used in school, in a store, or on the street? Be sure everyone agrees on the meanings of the expressions you have listed.

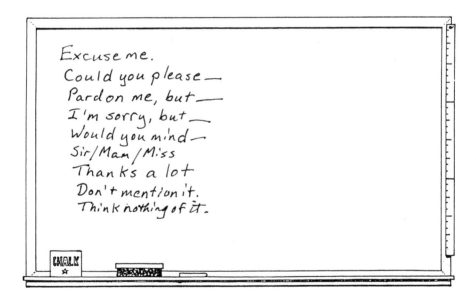

10. Sharpening a Pencil

Materials   pencils, a pencil sharpener, sheets of paper

Key words

an end	to turn	to put	to see
a hole	to keep	to take	sharp
a crank	to try	to look	firmly
a pencil sharpener	to hold		

Operation

1. Hold the pencil.
2. Put the end of the pencil into the hole of the pencil sharpener.
3. Hold the pencil firmly in the pencil sharpener.
4. Turn the crank with your right hand.
5. Keep turning the crank until the pencil is sharp.
6. Take the pencil out of the pencil sharpener.
7. Look to see if it is sharp.
8. Try writing on a sheet of paper with it.

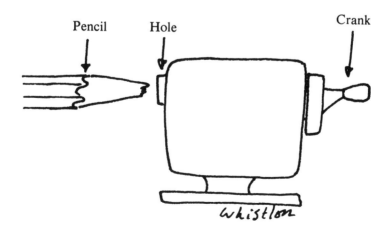

Pencil   Hole   Crank

whistlon

Grammar notes

-ing phrases — *turning, writing*
infinitive phrase — *to see*
until clause
if clause

Follow-up

1. After each step, Student A asks a *different* question. For example: *Where is the pencil? Where is the hole? How did you hold the pencil?* Student B answers the questions.

2. Student A gives directions and Student B follows them. When the operation is finished, Student A asks, *What did you do?* Student B explains the complete process in the past tense. Change roles and do it again.

3. Rewrite the operation, adding adverbs to those steps that don't have any. For instance: *tightly, completely, carefully, slowly, rapidly.*

4. Write an operation for sharpening a pencil with an electric pencil sharpener.

11. Operating a Cassette Recorder

Materials a cassette recorder, a cassette

Key words

a recorder	a battery	to insert	to push
a button	a tape	to advance	to open
a cassette	to plug in	to rewind	to listen
a cover	to eject	to play	forward
		to record	

Operation

1. Plug in the recorder (or check the batteries).
2. Push the Eject button to open the recorder.
3. Insert a cassette and close the cover.
4. Push the Fast Forward button to advance the tape and then stop.
5. Push the Play and Record buttons to record.
6. Say something.
7. Push the Stop button.
8. Push the Rewind button to rewind the tape.
9. Push the Play button to listen.

Grammar notes

infinitive phrases of purpose— *to open, to advance*
verbs used as adjectives — *eject button*

Follow-up

1. Use the recorder to record this operation or another one — for example, Operation 62.
2. Tape another pair of students, transcribe their operation exactly, and correct any grammar mistakes.
3. Write out the steps for operating a video cassette player.

12. Making a Paper Hat

Materials   paper

Key words

the bottom	to fold	to turn over	left
the center	to unfold	in half	right
a corner	to bring	folded	rectangular
a sheet		once	

Operation

1. Fold the paper in half with the folded edge up.
2. Fold the paper in half from left to right.
3. Unfold the paper once, leaving a line down the center and a fold at the top.
4. Bring the top right corner to the center line.
5. Bring the top left corner to the center line.
6. Fold the top sheet of the bottom rectangular piece up.
7. Turn the hat over.
8. Fold the other bottom piece up.

Grammar notes

adjectives in a series — *top right corner*
directional phrases — *from left to right*
-ing phrase — *leaving*
-ed adjective—*folded*

Follow-up

1. After the operation is completed, practice using questions such as, *How many times did you fold the paper? How did you make the hat?*

2. Write an original operation explaining how to make something out of paper. (Note operations 12 and 18.)

3. Unfold the hat by giving the directions in reverse order.

13. Making a Paper Airplane

Materials   sheets of paper

Key words

an edge	an illustration	to turn over	to test
a crease	to fold	to repeat	to produce
a point	to crease	to make	in half
a wing	to bring	to fly	lengthwise

Operation

1. Fold a sheet of paper in half lengthwise with the folded edge down.
2. Bring one top edge down to the crease and fold.
3. Turn over and repeat on the other side.
4. Fold again, bringing the upper folded corner, point A, down to point B (see illustration), and crease.
5. Repeat on the other side.
6. Make a lengthwise fold to produce a wing.
7. Repeat on the other side.
8. Fly the airplane to test it.

Grammar notes

infinitive phrases — *to produce, to test*
-*ing* phrase — *bringing*

Follow-up

1. Have a contest to see whose airplane will fly the highest and the longest distance.

2. Rewrite the operation as a paragraph. Use transition words such as, *first, second, then,* and *next.*

3. Write a story about an airplane, such as An Airplane Crash or Brandon's First Flight.

14. Making an Origami Cicada

Materials　Origami paper

Key words

a cicada	a line	to bring	to cover	diagonally
a point	to fold	to do	to make	along

Operation

1. Fold square ABCD diagonally along line DB.
2. Bring points B and D to point A(C), folding along lines XY and ZY.
3. Fold point D down near point Y along line XQ.
4. Do the same for point B on the other side by folding along QZ.
5. Folding along line RS, bring point C down to cover point Q.
6. Fold line RS down past line XZ, but not past point C.
7. Fold points X and Z behind along lines MN and OP.
8. Fold point A behind along line TU.
9. Fold points T and U back to make the cicada's eyes.

Grammar notes

adverbs of direction — *along, down, past, back, behind, back*
infinitive phrase — *to cover*
prepositional phrase of manner—*by folding*

Follow-up

1. Instead of doing this operation with Student A instructing Student B, Student A and B can work as a team to make the cicada as a problem-solving activity.
2. Find a friend from Japan and ask for additional origami.

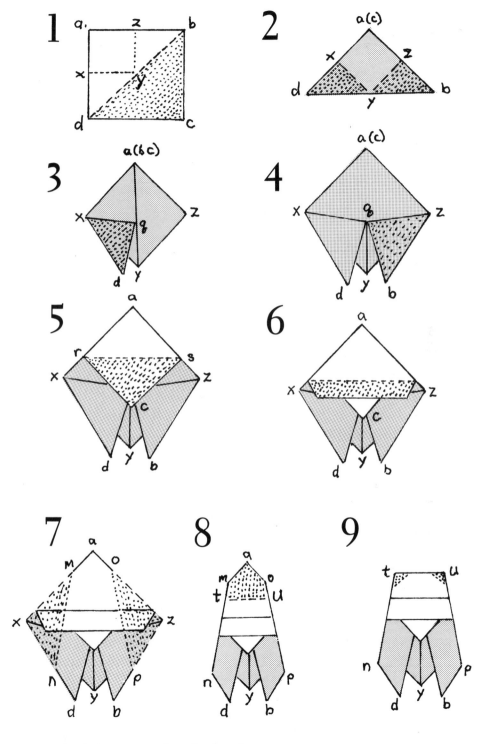

Shaded areas = colored side of paper

15. Having Fun with Rhymes

Materials   rhymes on page 33

Key words

a rhyme	a line	to choose	to ask
a title	aloud	to read	

Operation

1. Choose a rhyme from page 33.
2. What is the title of the rhyme? (Student B responds.)
3. How many lines are in the rhyme? (Student B responds.)
4. Please read the rhyme aloud. (Student B reads the rhyme aloud.)
5. Are there any words that you don't know? (Student B responds.)
6. If so, ask the teacher. (Student B asks the teacher.)
7. Please read the rhyme again. (Student B reads the rhyme again.)
8. What do you think this rhyme is about? (B interprets the rhyme.)

Grammar notes

Wh questions — *what, how many*
of phrase showing possession
yes/no question

Follow-up

1. Students A and B write questions about one of the rhymes. For example: *What did you like about this rhyme? Where did Humpty Dumpty sit?* After you have finished writing your questions, A asks B all of her questions and B responds. Then B asks all her questions and A responds.

2. Select one of the rhymes and draw illustrations for it.

3. Choose some rhymes and mark the heavily stressed syllables: **Húmpty Dúmpty sát on a wáll**. Read aloud with strong rhythm.

Humpty Dumpty

Humpty Dumpty sat on a wall.
Humpty Dumpty had a great fall.
All the King's horses and all the King's men
Couldn't put Humpty together again.

Little Boy Blue

Little Boy Blue, come blow your horn.
The sheep's in the meadow. The cow's in the corn.
Where's the little boy who looks after the sheep?
Under the haystack, fast asleep.

Rain

Rain, rain, go away,
Come again another day.
Little Johnny wants to play.

Jack and Jill

Jack and Jill went up the hill
To fetch a pail of water.
Jack fell down, and broke his crown,
And Jill came tumbling after.

The Cat and the Fiddle

Hey, diddle, diddle!
The cat and the fiddle.
The cow jumped over the moon.
The little dog laughed
To see such sport,
And the dish ran away with the spoon.

Peter Piper

Peter Piper picked a peck of pickled peppers.
A peck of pickled peppers Peter Piper picked.
If Peter Piper picked a peck of pickled peppers,
Where's the peck of pickled peppers Peter Piper picked?

Jack Be Nimble

Jack be nimble.
Jack be quick.
Jack jump over the candlestick.

Polly Put the Kettle On

Polly put the kettle on,
Polly put the kettle on,
Polly put the kettle on,
We'll all have tea.
Suky take it off again,
Suky take it off again,
Suky take it off again,
They've all gone away.

Little Bo Peep

Little Bo Peep has lost her sheep
And doesn't know where to find them.
Leave them alone and they'll come home
Wagging their tails behind them.

Jack Sprat

Jack Sprat could eat no fat,
His wife could eat no lean.
And so, between them both,
They licked the platter clean.

Georgie Porgie

Georgie Porgie, pudding and pie,
Kissed the girls and made them cry.
When the boys came out to play,
Georgie Porgie ran away.

When I Was Going up the Stair

When I was going up the stair
I met a man who wasn't there.
He wasn't there again today —
I wish that he would go away.

Dr. Foster

Dr. Foster
Went to Gloucester
In a shower of rain.
Fell into a puddle
Right up to his middle,
And never went there again.

Mistress Mary, Quite Contrary

Mistress Mary, quite contrary,
How does your garden grow?
With silver bells and cockleshells
And pretty maids all in a row.

Ride a Cock Horse

Ride a cock horse to Banbury Cross
To see a fine lady upon a white horse.
With rings on her fingers and bells on her toes,
She shall have music wherever she goes.

Wee Willie Winkie

Wee Willie Winkie ran through the town
Upstairs and downstairs in his nightgown,
Rapping on the windows,
Crying through the lock.
Are all the children in their beds,
For now it's nine o'clock?

16. Having Fun with Poetry

Materials   two copies of the same poetry book* or of the same poem for each pair of students (Emily Dickenson or e.e cummings work well). Each pair can have different material; you do not need a class set.

Key words

the table of contents	a poem to select	to take to open	to turn to read	to like short/long

Operation
1. Take the book.
2. Open it to the table of contents.
3. Select a poem.
4. Which poem did you select? (Student B responds.)
5. Turn to the poem. (Both students turn to the poem.)
6. Is it short or long? (Student B responds.)
7. Please read the poem. (Student B reads the poem.)
8. Did you like it? (Student B responds.)
9. What do(n't) you like about it? (Student B responds.)

Grammar notes

Wh questions
shift from *a* to *the*
yes/no questions

Follow-up
1. Create your own questions for steps 4, 6, 8 and 9.
2. Do the operation again, but this time Student A asks B questions based on the poem that B has selected. For example, A might ask, *What do you think the poet meant by* _____?

*By having two books, both Student A and B can find the poem. This enables A to ask questions that are specific to that particular poem. In addition, by finding different poems every time the operation is used, students vary the responses to the questions.

HOUSEHOLD ACTIVITIES

17. Lighting a Candle

Materials   matchbooks or matchboxes, candles

Key words

a matchbook	a wick	to strike	to hold
a candle	to tear out	to blow out	to close
a flame	to light	to throw away	to take out

Operation

1. Open the matchbook/matchbox.
2. Tear/take out a match.
3. Close the matchbook/matchbox.
4. Strike the match.
5. Hold the flame to the candle wick.
6. Light the candle.
7. Blow out the match.
8. Throw away the match.

①

②

③

Grammar notes

phrasal verbs—*blow out, throw away*

Follow-up

1. After Student A has read each step, Student B checks her comprehension by asking, *Should I (open the matchbook)*? Student A answers, and then Student B completes the action.

2. Do the operation again and use ordinal numbers. For example, Student A says, *First, open the matchbook. Second. . . .* Continue until the operation is completed. Change roles.

3. Practice with *What.* Student A asks, **What should I do first?** Student B says, *You should open the matchbook.* Student A opens the match book and then asks, **What do I do next?** Student B answers, and so on.

4. Do the operation again, separating the two parts of the phrasal verbs. For example: *take the match out.*

5. Relate the operation in the past tense. It has several irregular verbs.

18. Setting a Table

Materials   placemat, plate, teaspoon, knife, fork, glass, napkin

Key words

a plate	a napkin	a fork	to place
the center	a knife	the tip	to set
a placemat	a teaspoon	a glass	to put
the left-hand side		to fold	

Operation

1. Put the plate in the center of the placemat.
2. Fold the napkin.
3. Put the napkin to the left of the plate.
4. Place the knife to the right of the plate.
5. Put the teaspoon to the right of the knife.
6. Put the fork on the left-hand side of the plate, on top of the napkin.
7. Set the glass near the tip of the knife.

Grammar notes

locative phrases — *in the center, to the left*

Follow-up

1. Close your books. Student A completes the operation without interruption. She tells what she is doing **while** she is doing it. For example, *I'm putting the plate in the center of....* Changes roles.

2. Close your books. Student A completes the operation without interruption. Student B describes what she is doing, using as many tenses as she can. *She's putting the plate in the center of the placemat. Now she's going to . . .* and so on.

3. Create a silly place setting. Close your eyes and describe it to your partner. Then open them again to see if she has followed your directions correctly.

19. Setting an Alarm Clock

Materials   alarm clock

Key words

an alarm clock	an alarm hand	to wind	to ring
an hour hand	an alarm button	to set	to push in
a minute hand		to pull out	to get out of

Operation

1. Wind the alarm clock.
2. Set the hour and minute hands at the correct time.
3. Set the alarm hand for 7:00.
4. Pull out the alarm button.
5. When the alarm rings, push in the alarm button.
6. Get out of bed.

Grammar notes

compound nouns — *alarm clock, minute hand*
verbs that take particular prepositions — *set at, set for*

Follow-up

1. Write five questions that relate to the operation, such as: *Why do you use an alarm clock? When do you get up?* Then ask another student your questions. When finished, change roles.

2. Complete the following story: *Jennifer is always late for class in the morning. She tells her teacher that she is late because she doesn't have an alarm clock. Finally, Jennifer buys an alarm clock, but she doesn't know how to use it. Her friend Eleanor says, "I'll tell you how to use an alarm clock. First, you . . ."*

3. Bring in a digital alarm clock. Write an operation on setting the alarm. Divide into pairs. Give your partner the alarm clock. Read the directions, telling your partner how to set your alarm clock.

20. Threading a Needle

Materials   a needle, some thread, some buttons

Key words

a needle	an eye	to tie	to pull
a thumb	a knot	to hold	to make
a thread	to moisten	to put	

Operation

1. Hold the needle between your thumb and first finger.
2. Hold the thread in your other hand.
3. Moisten one end of the thread with your mouth.
4. Put the thread through the eye of the needle.
5. Pull the thread through.
6. Tie a knot in one end of the thread.
7. Make the knotted end longer than the other end.

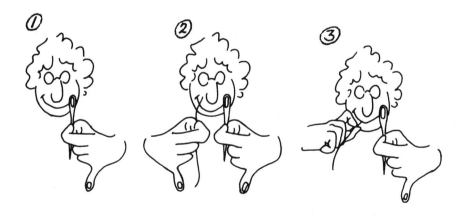

Grammar notes

locative phrases — *between your thumb, in one hand*
comparatives — *longer than*
the use of *one* and *the other*
-ed adjective — *knotted*

Follow-up

1. Student A gives directions and Student B follows them. When the operation is completed, Student A asks, *What did you do?* Student B explains the complete process in the past tense. Change roles and do it again.

2. Complete the following story: *Mrs. Anderson is teaching her son how to thread a needle. He soon will leave for college, and she wants him to be able to mend his clothes and sew on buttons. She says, "First, you hold the needle. . . ."*

3. Do operation 21.

4. Invent an operation for sewing a torn piece of cloth. Divide into pairs and practice it.

21. Sewing On a Button

Materials   buttons, needles, fabric, thread

Key words

frabic	a button	to sew	to hold
a needle	a hole	to thread	to pull
a knot	tightly	to tie	to bring
a thread		to cut	to repeat

Operation

1. Thread the needle.
2. Tie a knot in the end of the thread.
3. Hold the button on the fabric.
4. Pull the needle through the fabric and one of the holes in the button.
5. Bring the needle back through another hole.
6. Repeat until the button is on tightly.
7. Tie a knot in the thread.
8. Cut the thread.

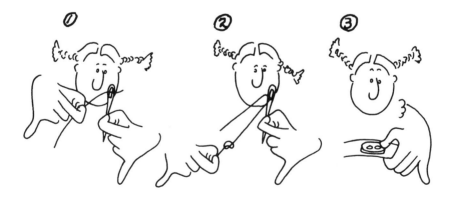

Grammar notes

locative phrases — *in the end, on the fabric*
until clause

Follow-up

1. Go through the sequence again in the past tense with Student A asking, *What did you do first/next?* and Student B answering in the past tense.

2. Go through the sequence using *going to.* Student A asks, *What are you going to do first/next?*

3. Find someone who knows how to knit, and write an operation for knitting.

22. Pounding a Nail

Materials   nails, a hammer, wood

Key words

wood	a hammer	to pick up	to continue
a thumb	a head	to hold	sharp
a finger	an end	to hit	secure
a nail	a handle	to remove	

Operation

1. Pick up the nail with one hand.
2. Hold it between your thumb and first finger.
3. Pick up the hammer with your other hand.
4. Hold it at the end of its handle.
5. Put the sharp end of the nail against the wood.
6. Hit the head of the nail with the hammer.
7. Remove your fingers when the nail is secure.
8. Continue hitting the head until the nail is hammered into the wood.

Grammar notes

locative phrases — *between your thumb and first finger, at the end of* phrases showing possession — *of its handle, of the nail*
time clauses — *until, when*
possessive adjectives — *its, your*
passive voice — *is hammered*

Follow-up

1. Rewrite the operation and add adjectives or adverbs. Here are some: *tight, careful, gentle, sharp.*

2. Do the entire operation in the passive voice as a narration. Begin with, *The nail is held with one hand.*

3. Write an operation for using a saw or some other tool.

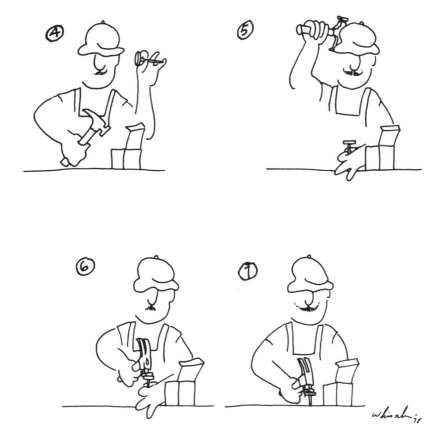

23. Potting a Plant

Materials   a pot, some soil, small stones, water

Key words

soil	to pot	to drain	excess	carefully
a stone	to press	to place	gently	slowly
a pot	to fill	to let	firmly	half full
a plant	to water			

Operation

1. Put some stones gently into the pot.
2. Fill the pot half full with soil.
3. Place the plant firmly into the soil.
4. Fill the pot up carefully with soil.
5. Press the soil firmly around the plant.
6. Water the plant slowly.
7. Let the excess water drain out of the pot.

Grammar notes

adverbs of manner — *gently, firmly*
count and noncount nouns — *stones, soil*
shift from no article to the definite article — *soil, the soil*

Follow-up

1. Do it as a dictation. Student A reads the operation to Student B. Student B writes down what Student A says. After you're finished, check your work with your book. Change roles and do it again.

2. Write the operation in narrative form in the past tense. For example: *Yesterday Jeffrey potted a plant. He put some stones gently into the pot and filled. . . .*

24. Changing Batteries in a Flashlight

Materials   flashlight, batteries

Key words

a flashlight	to unscrew	to put	to throw away
an end	to screw	to find	positive
a battery	to dump	to turn on	negative
a bulb			

Operation

1. Unscrew the flashlight.
2. Dump the old batteries into your hand.
3. Put them aside.
4. Find the positive (+) and negative (–) signs on the new batteries.
5. Put the two new batteries into the flashlight with the positive ends toward the bulb.
6. Screw the flashlight back together.
7. Turn the flashlight on to make sure that it works.
8. Throw the old batteries away.

Grammar notes

phrasal verbs — *turn on, throw away*
locative and directional prepositional phrases — *into your hand*
adverbs of direction — *aside, back on, away*

Follow-up

1. Do the operation as a dictation. Student A reads the operation to Student B. Student B writes down what Student A says. After you're finished, check your work with your book. Change roles and do it again.

2. Bring in something from home that has batteries in it. For example: *a camera, clock, toy, Walkman, tape recorder.* Write an operation for putting the batteries into the object. Then give the object and batteries to a partner and read the operation step by step so your partner can complete the operation.

25. Greeting a Guest

Materials   none

Key words

directions	to knock	to invite	glad
a pleasure	to open	to meet	nice
trouble	to come in	clear	

Operation: Dialogue Sequence

(Student A knocks on the door.)

(Student B opens the door.)

Student B: (*Student A's name*), *please come in.*

Student A: *Thanks.* (walks in)

Student B: *Did you have any trouble with the directions?*

Student A: *No trouble. In fact, they were very clear.*

Student B: *Good. I'm so glad that you were able to come.*

Student A: *Thanks. It's really nice of you to invite me.*

Student B: *My pleasure. Now come in and meet . . .*

Grammar notes

phrasal verb — *come in*
yes/no questions
adverbs modifying adjectives —*very, so, really*
Wh questions
that clause

Follow-up

1. Rewrite the dialogue as an operation, first for the host and then for the guest. For example, begin with 1. *Open the door.*

2. Students can explore cross-cultural differences in greetings. Working in pairs with students from other countries, students write two dialogue sequences — one dialogue sequence for Student A's country and one for Student B's country. The sequences should be in English. When they're finished, each pair role-plays the dialogues for the rest of the class.

3. Discuss cultural differences in time as it relates to dinner and party invitations. How long before an event are guests invited? What are polite arrival and departure times? Discuss other cultural practices related to entertaining. When do guests bring gifts? What kinds of gifts are appropriate? When are the gifts opened? How many times will the host offer drinks? How much food should a guest eat? What else does someone need to know about being a guest in your country?

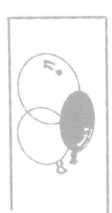

GAMES AND EXERCISES

26. Blowing Up a Ballon

Materials   balloons

Key words

a balloon	to stretch	to tie	to hold
an end	to blow up	to put	full
a knot	to escape	to take out	

Operation

1. Stretch the balloon.
2. Put the open end into your mouth.
3. Blow up the balloon until it's full.
4. Take it out of your mouth.
5. Hold the end together so that the air doesn't escape.
6. Tie a knot in the end of the balloon.

Grammar notes

locative phrase — *in the end*
until clause
so that clause
formation of contracted negatives — *doesn't*
contracted *be* — *it's*

Follow-up

1. Close your books. Student A gives the directions. When the operation is completed, Student A asks, *What did you do?* Student B explains the process. Change roles and do it again.
2. Write some variations that involve bursting balloons, releasing balloons, shaping balloons.
3. Describe the action as classmates play "Volleyballoon."
4. Discuss the typical order of events at a birthday party.

27. Hopping on One Leg

Materials   none

Key words

an ankle	to bend	to hop	once
a time	to grab	to let go of	apart
to stand	to raise	to put	

Operation

1. Stand with both your feet one foot apart.
2. Bend your left knee.
3. Raise your left foot behind you.
4. Grab your left ankle with your left hand.
5. Hop five times.
6. Let go of your ankle.
7. Put your foot back on the floor.
8. Hop once on both your feet.

Grammar notes

word order with determiners and adjectives — *both your feet*

Follow-up

1. Do the operation again, and add transition words and phrases. For example: *First stand on both feet. Now bend your left knee. OK, next you're ready to raise. . . .*

2. Write one or more additional operations with these words: *step, walk, skip, jump, leap, march, stroll, sidestep, stride.*

3. Student A writes each step of two or more operations on a separate piece of paper and then mixes the pieces up and gives them to Student B. Student B separates the operations and puts the steps in their correct order and then reads them to Student A. Student A follows the directions.

4. Ask your teacher if she knows how to do "the hanky panky."

28. Touching Your Toes

Materials   none

Key words

a waist	to place	to keep	to drop
a knee	to bend down	to straighten up	to raise
to stand up	to touch	to bring	apart

Operation

1. Stand up.
2. Place your feet a foot apart.
3. Raise your arms up over your head.
4. Bend down from the waist and ...
5. Touch your toes with your fingers.
6. Keep your knees straight.
7. Straighten up and bring your hands to your waist.
8. Drop your hands to your sides.

Grammar notes

possessive adjective — *your*
directional phrases — *from the waist*
compound sentence — *bend down and touch*

Follow-up

1. Lead the class in a four-count exercise (steps 3, 4 + 5 + 6, 7, 8) saying just: *raise, bend and touch, straighten and bring, drop, raise*, etc. Do it to music.

2. Write an operation on doing sit-ups (or another fitness exercise). Perform the operation in pairs.

3. After you complete the operation, write five questions that relate to it, such as: *Where were your feet? Did you keep your knees straight?* Then ask your partner the questions. Your partner answers the questions and then asks her questions.

29. Playing "Would You Please"

(a variation of "Simon Says")

Materials   none

Key words   would you please   to touch   to turn around
                would you mind   to jump

Note: The teacher introduces the game to the class by giving directions and asking the whole class to respond. When she says, **Would you please** *touch your nose?* or **Would you mind** *touching your nose?*, the students follow the directions. When the teacher does *not* say **Would you please . . . ?** or **Would you mind . . . ?**, the students do *not* complete the action. When students understand the game, they can practice in pairs.

Operation

1. Student A: *Would you mind touching the floor?*
2. Student B touches the floor.
3. Student A: *Would you please jump up and down three times?*
4. Student B jumps up and down three times.
5. Student A: *Would you please turn around?*
6. Student B turns around.
7. Student A: *Touch your toes.*
8. Student B does *not* touch her toes.

Grammar notes

would you please + bare infinitive
would you mind + gerund
possessive adjective — *your*
directional adverbs — *up and down, around*

Follow-up

1. After you have practiced in pairs, a volunteer can lead the whole class in a game. You should close your books and listen to the student in front of the class. The student who misses (follows a command that does not include the words *Would you mind . . . ?* or *Would you please . . . ?*) becomes the leader and goes to the front of the class. The leader may vary the instructions. For example: *Stick your finger in your ear.* Creative commands lead to more fun.
2. Operations 27 and 28 can be used with "Would you please."

30. Playing Jacks

Materials   jacks, a small rubber ball

Key words

a jack	to bounce	to put	to pick up
to throw	to catch	to let	one at a time
to toss	to repeat		

Operation

1. Throw the jacks onto the floor.
2. Toss the ball into the air.
3. Pick up one jack before the ball bounces.
4. Let the ball bounce once.
5. Catch the ball with the same hand.
6. Put the jack into your other hand.
7. Repeat until you've picked up all the jacks, one at a time.

Grammar notes

time clauses — *before, until*
directional phrases — *onto the floor, into the air*
let + noun phrase + bare infinitive
use of *one* and *the other*

Follow-up

1. Do it as a dictation. Student A reads the operation to Student B. Student B writes down what Student A says. After you're finished, check your work with your text. Change roles and do it again.

2. Close your books. Student A completes the operation. She tells what she is doing *while* she is doing it. When she's finished, Student B completes the operation in the same way.

3. Close your books. Student A completes the operation. Student B describes what she is doing while she is doing it. She uses as many tenses as she can. For instance: *She is throwing the jacks onto the floor. Now she's just . . . She's going to. . .* , and so on.

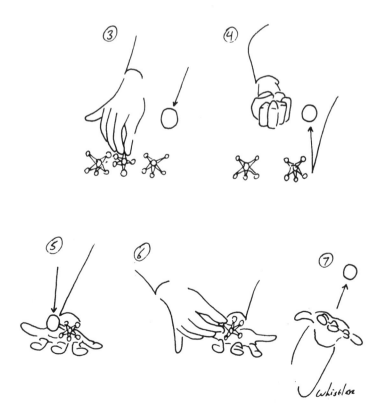

31. Playing Dice

Score Sheet
2
3
4
5
6
7
8
9
10
11
12

Materials   dice   **Note:** To be played in groups of 2 or 3

Key words	a player	to pick up
a score sheet	a step	to count
the dice	to check	to give
a dot	to throw	to tell
a check mark	to put	to continue

Operation

1. Pick up two dice.
2. Throw the dice on top of the desk.
3. Count the number of dots on top of the dice.
4. Put a check mark after the same number on the score sheet.
5. Give the dice to the next player.
6. Tell her to do steps one through six.
7. Continue until you have checked all the numbers.

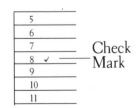

5	
6	
7	Check
8 ✓	Mark
9	
10	
11	

Grammar notes

locative phrases — *after the number, on the score sheet*
verbs that take particular preposition — *give to*
compound nouns — *score sheet*
until clause

Follow-up

1. Write an operation on playing a different game of dice.
2. Write an operation for playing dominoes.

32. Negotiating an Invitation To Play

Materials   none

Key words

would like to   to negotiate   can
would love to   to play   have to

Operation: Dialogue Sequence

Student A: *Hey, (Student B's name). Would you like to play*
_____ this afternoon?

Student B: *I'd love to play, but I have to* _____.

Student A: *OK, how about* _____?

Student B: *I can't play then either. I have to* _____.

Student A: *Maybe this weekend?*

Student B: *I'm* _____. *How about* _____?

Student A: *Great!* _____ *o'clock?*

Student B: _____ *o'clock.*

Grammar notes

would like/love to
modals — *can't, have to*
adverbs of time — *this afternoon, tomorrow*
how about question

Follow-up

Students can explore cross-cultural differences in negotiating invitations. Working in pairs with students from other countries, students write two dialogue sequences — one dialogue sequence for Student A's country and one for Student B's country. One student invites the other to participate in a sports event. The student being invited has a conflicting engagement. They negotiate a time that is agreeable to them both. The sequences should be in English. When they're finished, each pair role-plays the dialogues for the rest of the class.

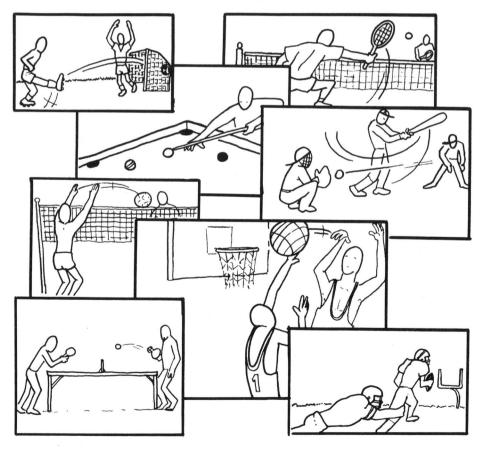

FOOD AND RECIPES

33. Eating Cookies

Materials   a box of cookies in a bag

Key words

a bag	a cookie	to take out	to close
a box	to open	to eat	another

Operation

1. Take the bag.
2. Open the bag.
3. Take out the box.
4. Open the box.
5. Take a cookie.
6. Eat the cookie.
7. Take another one.
8. Close the box.

Grammar notes

the use of *one* as a noun substitute
shift from *a* to *the*

Follow-up

Close your books and sit in a circle. Pass the bag of cookies around the circle. Each student says the operation to the student next to her. Continue until the bag of cookies has been passed completely around the circle.

34. Eating an Apple

Materials   apples, water, towels, knives

Key words

an apple	to wash	to put	to take away
a mouth	to wipe	to bite	dry
a tooth, teeth	to hold	to chew	
	to open	to swallow	

Operation

1. Wash the apple.
2. Wipe it dry.
3. Hold it in your hand.
4. Open your mouth.
5. Put the apple between your teeth.
6. Bite into it.
7. Take the apple away from your mouth.
8. Chew and swallow.

Grammar notes

the object pronoun *it*
possessive adjective — *your*

Follow-up

1. Write an operation on eating a banana.
2. Write an operation on peeling an apple. Divide into pairs and perform the operation. Try to peel it so that the peel comes off in one unbroken strip.
3. Write an operation for cutting up the apple and taking out the core. Perform the operation in pairs.

35. Chewing Gum

Materials   packs of gum

Key words

gum	to open	to swallow
a pack	to unwrap	to chew
a piece	to throw away	to put
	to pull out	

Operation

1. Open the pack of gum.

2. Pull out a piece of gum.

3. Unwrap the piece of gum.

4. Put the gum in your mouth.

5. Chew it.

6. Do not swallow it.

7. Throw away the paper.

Grammar notes

shift from *a* to *the*
phrasal quantifiers — *pack of, piece of*
negative imperative
phrasal verbs — *pull out, throw away*
countable and uncountable nouns — *a pack, gum*

Follow-up

1. Rewrite the operation and add an adjective to steps 1, 2, 3, and 7. For example: *Open the pack of **chewing** gum.*

2. Rewrite the operation and add an adverb to steps 1, 2, 3, 4, 5, and 7. For example: ***Quickly** open the pack of gum.*

3. In pairs, practice prepositions of location. Student A gives Student B directions and Student B follows them. For example, Student A says, *Put a stick of gum on the desk. Now put the gum next to your pencil.* The teacher can provide a list of prepositions.

36. Making a Cup of Instant Coffee

Materials   instant coffee, cups, spoons, milk, sugar, water, hot plate

Key words

coffee	a cup	to put	to add
milk	to boil	to stir	boiling
sugar	to fill		

Operation

1. Boil some water.

2. Put some coffee into your cup.

3. Fill the cup with boiling water.

4. Stir the coffee.

5. Add some milk to the coffee.

6. Add some sugar.

7. Stir the coffee again.

Grammar notes

count and noncount nouns — *a cup, some water*
the use of *some* and *the*
verbs that take particular prepositions — *add **to**, fill **with***
-*ing* adjective — *boiling*

Follow-up

1. As Student A completes the operation, Student B describes what Student A is doing. For example: *You're boiling some water. Now you're putting some coffee ....*

2. While Student A performs the operation, Student B talks about what Student A is doing, using as many tenses as she can. For example: *She **has** just **put** the water into .... Soon the water **will** .... Now she is. ...*

3. Write an operation on making tea.

37. Making Instant Pudding

Materials   a package of instant pudding, milk, a bowl, spoons, serving bowls

Key words

directions	a package	an amount	to open	to add
contents	a mixture	to stir	to pour	to allow
pudding	a bowl	to read	to eat	to thicken

Operation

1. Read the directions on the pudding package.
2. Open the package and pour the contents into a bowl.
3. Add the correct amount of milk.
4. Stir the mixture together.
5. Pour it into individual bowls.
6. Allow it to thicken.
7. Eat it.

Grammar notes

the object pronoun *it*
locative phrase — *on the package*
directional phrase — *into a bowl*

Follow-up

1. Do it as a dictation. Student A reads the operation to Student B. Student B writes down what Student A says. After you're finished, check your work with your book. Change roles and do it again.

2. Investigate the American measurement system (*cup, teaspoon*).

3. Write another operation for an instant food. For example: *soup, mashed potatoes, rice, cake mix.*

whistler

38. Making a
Peanut Butter and Jelly Sandwich

Materials   a loaf of bread, a jar of peanut butter, a jar of jelly, a knife

Key words

peanut butter	a slice	a lid	to spread	to put
jelly	a package	a sandwich	to screw	to cut
bread	a jar	to take	to unscrew	in half

Operation

1. Take two slices of bread from the package.
2. Unscrew the lid of the peanut butter jar.
3. Unscrew the lid of the jelly jar.
4. Spread the peanut butter on one slice of bread.
5. Spread the jelly on the other slice of bread.
6. Put the two slices of bread together.
7. Cut the sandwich in half.
8. Screw the lids onto the jars.

Grammar notes

count and noncount nouns — *a jar, jelly*
of phrases showing possession
use of *one* and *the other*

Follow-up

1. Student A writes each step of the operation on a separate piece of paper. Then she mixes them up and gives them to Student B. Student B puts the steps in their correct order and reads them to Student A. Student A follows the directions.

2. Write an operation for making a cheeseburger, a hot dog, a taco, a pizza, a sub, or some other sandwich type of food.

39. Making Spaghetti

Materials   stove or hot plate, large pan, water, spaghetti

Key words

spaghetti	to boil	to read	to turn on
directions	to stick	to fill	to wait for
a pan	to put in	to throw	on high
a burner	to let		

Operation

1. Read the directions on the spaghetti box.
2. Fill the pan almost full of water.
3. Turn the burner on high.
4. Wait for the water to boil.
5. Put in the spaghetti.
6. Let it boil for as long as the directions say.
7. Throw one piece of spaghetti against the wall.
8. If it sticks, the spaghetti is done.

Grammar notes

compound noun — *spaghetti box*
phrasal verb — *put in*
wait for + noun phrase + infinitive — *wait for the water to boil.*
let + noun phrase + bare infinitive
adverb of time — *as long as*
if clause
past participle used as adjective — *done*
phrasal quantifier — *piece of*

Follow-up

1. After you have successfully completed the operation and are familiar with the vocabulary and sentence structures, you can each write five *Wh* questions. For example: **Where are the directions?** Then ask and answer each other's questions.

2. Prepare directions for a complete spaghetti dinner.

40. Making Popcorn

Materials an air popcorn popper, popcorn, measuring cup, bowl, electrical outlet

Key words

popcorn	to pour	to unplug	to listen to
a popcorn popper	to plug in	to put	to eat
a measuring cup	to wait	to place	to pop

Operation

1. Put the correct amount of popcorn into a measuring cup.
2. Pour the popcorn into the popcorn popper.
3. Place a bowl in front of the popcorn popper.
4. Plug in the popcorn popper.
5. Wait.
6. Listen to the popcorn pop.
7. When the popcorn has finished popping, unplug the popcorn popper.
8. Eat the popcorn.

Grammar notes

locative and directional phrases
phrasal verb — *plug in*
when clause
compound nouns — *popcorn popper*

Follow-up

1. Divide into pairs. Student A reads the operation to Student B and adds transition words. For example: **First,** *put the correct amount of popcorn* . . . . **Then** *pour the popcorn* . . . .

2. Bring in needles and thread. Student A threads the needle and then strings popcorn by carefully pulling the threaded needle through the kernels of popcorn to make a "popcorn chain." As Student A is threading popcorn, Student B is telling her what she is doing. For example, Student B says, *You're putting the needle into the popcorn. Now you're pulling the needle out of the popcorn. You're pushing the popcorn down the string. The popcorn broke. You have to start again.*

41. Making Coffee in a Drip Coffeemaker

Materials   at least one drip coffeemaker, ground coffee, a coffee scoop, coffee filters

Key words

coffee	a pot	a filter	to open	to close	to take out
a coffeemaker	a scoop	to drip	to pour	to fill	to turn on

Operation

1. Open the "door" of the coffeemaker.
2. Put a coffee filter around the inside of the basket.
3. Put three scoops of coffee into the filter.
4. Close the "door."
5. Take out the glass pot.
6. Fill it with cold water to the six-cup mark.
7. Open the top of the coffeemaker and pour in the water.
8. Turn the coffeemaker on.
9. When the coffee finishes dripping, pour a cup of coffee.

Grammar notes

of possessive — **of** *the coffee maker*
locative phrases
shift from *a* to *the*
phrasal verbs — *take out, turn on*
when clause
phrasal quantifier — *scoops of*
finish + gerund — *finishes dripping*

Follow-up

1. After Student A has completed the operation, Student B asks, *What did you do?* Student A tells what she did, using the past tense. For example: *I opened the "door" of the coffeemaker.* After Student B completes the operation, Student A asks, *What did you do?* and Student B responds similarly.

2. Write this operation as a paragraph, using transition words such as *first, next,* and *now.* Combine some of the steps so you have only five sentences in the paragraph.

42. Ordering Coffee

Materials none (The teacher may bring in examples of decaffeinated and regular coffee, sweetener and sugar to explain the differences.)

Key words

cream	sugar	regular
sweetener	would you like . . .	decaf

Operation

Student A: *Would you like something to drink?*

Student B: *Coffee, please.*

Student A: *Regular or decaf?*

Student B: _____, *please.*

Student A: Cream and sugar or sweetener?

Student B: _____, please.

Student A: *Anything else?*

Student B: *No, that's all.*

Grammar notes

would you like + pronoun
noncount nouns

Follow-up

1. In pairs, use menus and write dialogue sequences for ordering food. When you're finished, you can role-play your dialogues in front of the class.

2. Students can conduct sociolinguistic research on ordering food in a restaurant. Each student goes to a restaurant (for example: fast food chains, campus cafes) and sits at a table where she can hear customers order food. Students write down the dialogues that they hear. They bring their results to class to report on what they heard.

43. Using a Fast Food Restaurant Drive-Through

Materials   fast food menus (optional) (This operation can be mimed.)

Key words

a menu	to drive	to open	to order	to take
a voice	to roll up	to wait	to pay for	to leave

Operation

1. Drive to the menu sign.
2. Open your window.
3. Wait for a voice.
4. Order your food when the voice asks, "What do you want?"
5. Drive to the pick-up window.
6. Pay for the food.
7. Take the food.
8. Roll up your window and leave.

Grammar notes

phrasal verbs — *roll up*	*when* clause	*Wh* question
shift from a to the	direct quotation	

Follow-up

1. Act this out as a role-play with Student A as the fast food employee and Student B as the customer. Write out a dialogue first and then rehearse it, eventually performing your role-play for the class. If you have fast food menus or coupons, use them.

2. Using props such as signs and menus, set the room up so it represents a strip of fast food restaurants. Each restaurant needs one student to play the part of the employee. The other students can "drive" from restaurant to restaurant ordering appropriate food such as tacos, hamburgers, chicken, or ice cream.

COMMUNICATION

44. Mailing a Letter

Materials   paper, envelopes, pens, stamps

Key words

a letter	the front	to fold	to put
an envelope	a return address	to lick	to write
a flap	a corner	to seal	upper left-hand
an address	a stamp	to mail	right-hand

Operation

1. Fold the letter to fit the envelope.
2. Put the letter in the envelope.
3. Lick the flap and seal the envelope.
4. Write the address on the front of the envelope.
5. Write the return address in the upper left-hand corner.
6. Lick the stamp.
7. Put the stamp in the upper right-hand corner.
8. Mail the letter.

Return Address

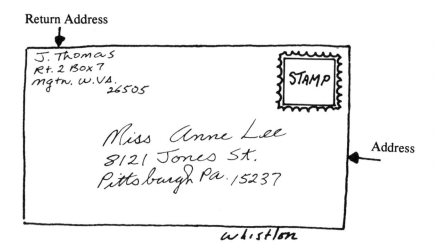

Address

Grammar notes

locative phrases — *in the envelope, in the corner*
infinitive phrase used as an adverb of manner — *to fit*

Follow-up

1. Divide into pairs and sit back to back. Student A gives Student B directions for drawing a postage stamp or a fully-addressed envelope. Student A follows the directions that she gives Student B, so that both students are drawing the same thing. Student A should be as detailed and specific as possible. For example: Student A says, *Draw an envelope that is 4 by 9 inches. In the upper right-hand corner, draw a . . . .* Both students follow the directions. Student B may ask questions but may not see Student A's picture until it is finished. When finished, compare pictures. Change roles and do it again.

2. Describe the format for addresses, envelopes, and letters in your country and compare with the illustration.

45. Using a Pay Telephone

Materials   a telephone (or a drawing of one), some coins

Key words

directions	a pay telephone	to pick up	to press
a telephone	a key	to insert	to listen
receiver	a dial tone	to hold	continuous

Operation

1. Read the directions.
2. Pick up the telephone receiver.
3. Hold it to your ear.
4. Insert the correct amount of money.
5. Listen for the dial tone, a continuous sound.
6. Press the keys of the number that you are calling.
7. Listen until someone answers on the other end.

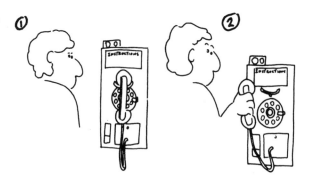

Grammar notes

noun phrase in apposition — *a continuous sound*
compound noun — *telephone receiver*
until clause
adjective (relative) clause — *the number **that you are calling***

Follow-up

1. Write this operation as a paragraph adding five adjective clauses. For example: *First, you read the directions that are written on the telephone....*

2. Write an operation on making a long-distance phone call, a collect call, or a call with a credit card.

3. Write an operation on sending a telegram by phone. Divide into pairs. Perform the operation. Student A dictates the message, and Student B writes it down. Compare the messages. Then reverse roles.

4. Practice leaving a message on an answering machine.

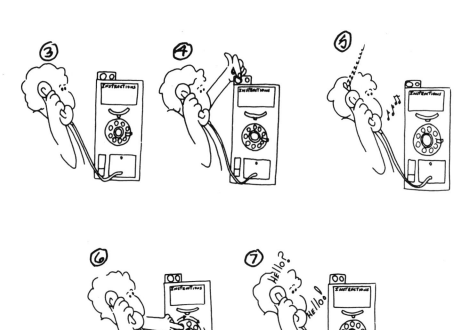

46. Using a Fax Machine

Materials   a fax machine (or a picture of one)*

Key words

a fax	an electronic	to feed	to send
a button	handshake	to press	to listen for
a display	to look over	to mark	to call
a sound	to fax	to punch	to receive
a message	to check	to report	face-down

Operation

1. Look over the message to be faxed to be sure it is ready.
2. Feed the paper face-down into the machine.
3. Press the button marked "dial."
4. Punch in the number you are calling.
5. Check the display to be sure it is correct.
6. If it is correct, press the button marked "send."
7. Listen for the sound called the electronic handshake.
8. Press the key marked "report" to be sure your message was received.

*Note: If necessary, adapt this option to your particular fax machine.

Grammar notes

infinitive phrase of purpose — *to be sure*
reduced adjective clause — *the button* (that is) *marked "dial"*
passive voice — *was received*
passive infinitive — *to be faxed*

Follow-up

1. Find and fill out a fax form.

2. Write out the steps of the operation and fax them to a friend who will correct them and fax them back.

3. Repeat the operation, expanding all the reduced clauses to full clauses: *The button marked* → *the button **that is** marked.*

4. Repeat the operation with the infinitive phrase first: *To be sure your message is ready, . . .*

5. Write out instructions for using a photocopier, starting up a computer, or using an answering machine.

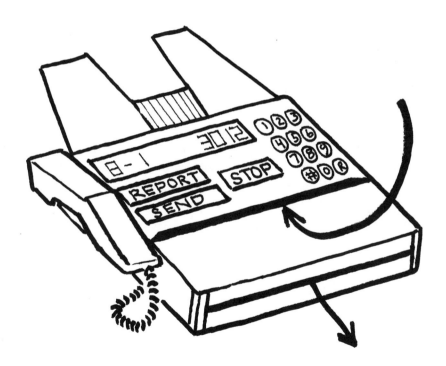

47. Wiring Money

Materials   a telephone book

Key words

Western Union	to look up	to go	to give
a phone book	to write down	to send	to pay
a money order form	to fill out	to tell	clearly
a charge	to wire	to print	carefully

Operation

1. Look up Western Union in the phone book.
2. Write down the address.
3. Go to the Western Union office with the cash that you want to send.
4. Tell the person at the office that you want to wire money.
5. Fill out the money order form.
6. Print clearly and carefully.
7. Give the person the money that you're sending.
8. Pay the charge for sending the money.

Grammar notes

phrasal verb — *to fill out*
adverbs of manner — *clearly, carefully*
that clause as noun clause — *tell the person **that you want to send money***
that clause as adjective clause — *the money **that you're sending***
compound noun — *phone book*
double object verbs — *tell, give*

Follow-up

1. Do this operation as a role-play, setting up a mock Western Union office in the classroom. Divide into groups of 3; Student A gives directions, and Students B and C role-play the operation. When completed, change roles and do it again.
2. Discuss other ways to send or receive money quickly.

Telegraphic Money Order Application

48. Phoning for Flight Information

Materials   none

Key words

a flight	to help	to leave	nonstop
a fare	to need	to arrive	in advance
a reservation	to travel	to return	may
to book	to plan	cheapest	must

Operation

Student A: _____ Airlines, (Student A's name) speaking. *How may I help you?*

Student B: *I need flight information on flying from* _____ *to* _____.

Student A: *When are you planning to travel?*

Student B: *I'm planning to leave* _____ *on*

_____.

Student A: *We have a nonstop flight that leaves at* _____ *and arrives at* _____. *It's flight number* _____.

Student B: *Sounds great.*

Student A: *When are you planning to return?*

Student B: *I'm returning on* _____.

Student A: *We have two flights. One at* _____ *and the other at* _____.

Student B: *Which is nonstop?*

Student A: *The* _____ *flight.*

Student B: *That's fine. What's the fare?*

Student A: *Our cheapest fare is* _____, *and reservations must be made* _____ *days in advance. May I book your reservation?*

Student B: *Yes, please.*

Grammar notes

Wh questions
infinitives — *to travel, to return*
one and *the other*
plan + infinitive
that clause
modals — *must, may*

Follow-up

1. Each student calls an airline to obtain flight information to another place. Specifically, you should find out the different costs of the flights depending on the kind of ticket you buy (*full fare, Saturday layover, excursion fare*). Report back to the class.

2. Scan the telephone directory and ask other people to find out what free services the phone company offers (calling for the time, the weather, long distance information). Report back to class on the free services and the phone numbers for those services. (For example: long distance information = 1 + area code + 555-1212.)

3. Write an operation based on the dialogue:
   1. *First, call a travel agent.*
   2. *When the agent answers, tell her . . . ,*etc.

4. Use the timetable below for additional practice with making reservations with a travel agent. Student A makes reservations with Travel Agent Student B.

SCHEDULE

AIRLINE	FLIGHT	DEPARTURE		ARRIVAL		
AMERICAN	108	BOSTON	7:30 PM	LONDON	6:50 AM	DAILY
BRITISH AIR	212	BOSTON	7:40 PM	LONDON	7:00 AM	DAILY
NORTHWEST	48	BOSTON	8:25 PM	LONDON	7:40 AM	DAILY
VIRGIN ATLANTIC	12	BOSTON	8:40 PM	LONDON	8:10 AM	TWFS
BRITISH AIR	213	LONDON	10:30 PM	BOSTON	1:05 PM	DAILY
AMERICAN	109	LONDON	11:30 PM	BOSTON	2:05 PM	DAILY
NORTHWEST	49	LONDON	12:25 PM	BOSTON	2:45 PM	DAILY
VIRGIN ATLANTIC	11	LONDON	3:00 PM	LONDON	5:10 PM	MTThF

MISCELLANEOUS ACTIVITIES

49. Writing a Check

Materials   pens or pencils

Key words

ink	a payee	a figure	a register	to make
a check	a transaction	a memo	to write	to record
a date line	an amount	a note	to sign	

Operation

1. Write today's date in ink on the date line.
2. Write the payee's name on the next line.
3. Write the amount of the check in figures.
4. Write the amount of the check in words.
5. Sign the check on the last line.
6. Make a note on the memo line.
7. Record the transaction in your check register.

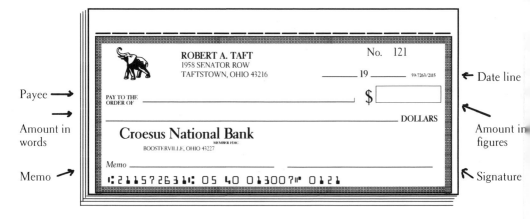

Grammar notes

locative phrases — *on the date line, in your check register*
's possessive — *today's date*
of possessive — *amount of the check*
manner adverbial — *in ink*

Follow-up

1. Write five questions that relate to the operation, such as: *What is the date? Where did you sign the check?* Then ask another student the questions. When finished, change roles.

2. Write the complete operation, using the words *after* and *before* with each pair of sentences: *After you write today's date . . . ,*etc.

ROBERT A. TAFT	No. 122
1958 SENATOR ROW	
TAFTSTOWN, OHIO 43216	_____ 19 _____ 59-7263/2115

PAY TO THE
ORDER OF _____ $ [   ]

_____ DOLLARS

Croesus National Bank
MEMBER FDIC
BOOSTERVILLE, OHIO 43227

Memo _____   _____

⑈2⑆572631⑈ 05 40 013007⑈ 0122

CHECK REGISTER RECORDS

RECORD ALL CHARGES OR CREDITS THAT AFFECT YOUR ACCOUNT

NUMBER	DATE	TRANSACTION DECRIPTION OR PAYEE NAME	(−) PAYMENT OR WITHDRAWAL		(+) DEPOSIT OR INTEREST	BALANCE $	

Note: You may copy the forms for practice.

50. Using an Umbrella

Materials   umbrellas

Key words

an umbrella	a rod	to push	to take
a tie	to undo	to remove	to put
a handle	to aim	to hold	

Operation

1. Take an umbrella.
2. Undo the tie.
3. Hold the handle with one hand.
4. Put the other hand on the rod of the umbrella.
5. Aim the umbrella straight in front of you.
6. Push your hand up the rod until the umbrella opens.
7. Remove your hand from the rod of the umbrella.
8. Hold the umbrella a few inches over your head.

Grammar notes

shift from *an* to *the*
use of *one* and *the other*
locative phrases — *on the rod, in front of*
until clause

Follow-up

1. Student A writes each step of the operation on a separate strip of paper, mixes them up, and gives them to Student B. Student B puts the steps in their correct order and reads them to Student A. Student A follows the directions.

2. Do it as a dictation. Student A reads the operation to Student B. Student B writes down what Student A says. After you're finished, check your work with your book. Change roles and do it again.

51. Using a Vending Machine

Materials   a vending machine (or a picture of one), coins

Key words

directions	a coin slot	to select	to read	to pull
change	a button	to push	to find	to take
a vending	a knob	to want	to put	exact
machine	a selection	to open	to buy	

Operation

1. Read the directions on the vending machine.
2. Select what you want to buy.
3. Find the coin slot.
4. Put the exact change into the coin slot.
5. Push the button for your selection.
6. Open the door or pull the knob.
7. Take your selection from the machine.

Grammar notes

locative phrase — *on the vending machine*
compound nouns — *vending machine, coin slot*
compound sentence with *or*

Follow-up

1. Write five questions that relate to the operation, such as: *"What did you buy? Where is the coin slot?"* Then ask another student your questions. That student replies to the questions. When finished, change roles.

2. List all the different things that are sold in vending machines. Discuss vending machines and American culture (fast foods and junk foods).

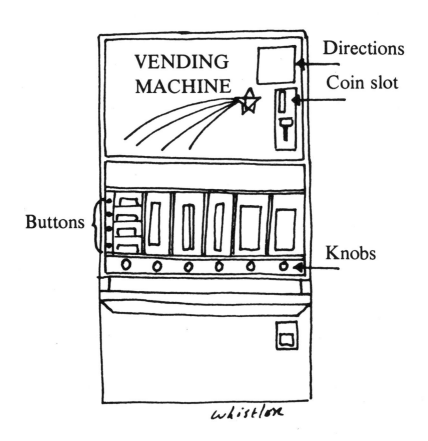

52. Filling In a Form

Materials   pens or pencils, copies of a form

Key words

directions	a form	to check	to read
a code	to fill in	to sign	to use
a rank	to write	to date	academic
a college			

Operation
1. Read the directions at the top of the form.
2. Fill in your student number and your name.
3. Read the codes at the bottom of the form.
4. Fill in your academic rank and college, using the numbers in the codes.
5. Use numbers to fill in your date of birth.
6. Write in all other information.
7. Check everything you have written.
8. Sign and date the form.

Grammar notes

locative phrases — *at the top, at the bottom*
phrasal verb — *fill in*
-*ing* phrase
infinitive phrase — *to fill in*

Follow-up
1. Pretend that you're going to study at an American university, and create student numbers, ranks, majors, colleges, and American addresses. After you've finished the operation, write a letter to your major department, and request specific information on the program that you're enrolling in.
2. Bring in real forms and rewrite the operation to match the forms (credit card applications, change of address cards, magazine subscriptions, bank account forms, and job application forms).

Admissions and Records Center
Student Information Form

AMERICAN UNIVERSITY   Admissions and Records Center

STUDENT INFORMATION FORM

Read these directions first!
1. Print data in the appropriate blocks in each box.
2. Use the codes below when coded information is required.
3. Do not go beyond the number of blocks provided (abbreviate if necessary)

Student Number

Student Name
last   first

Academic Rank (use code below)

Current Major

Academic College (see code below)

Sex
F=female
M=male

Marital Status
M=married
S=single

Date of birth
mo. day year

Local Street Address

Local City Address

State

Zip Code

Student's Signature   Date

Rank Codes	
Code	*Rank*
01	Freshman
02	Sophomore
03	Junior
04	Senior
05	Graduate Student

Schools and Colleges	
Code	*School or College*
07	Agriculture and Forestry
14	Arts and Sciences
21	Business and Economics
35	Engineering
42	Graduate
45	Education
80	Dentistry
83	Medicine
86	Nursing

Note: A *major* area of study is in a department within a *college*; for example, a history major is in the College of Arts and Sciences; and a business administration major is in the College of Business and Economics

53. Using a Self-Serve Gas Station

Materials   none (This operation can be done in pantomime.)

Key words

a gas station	a tank	to get out of	to put	to turn on
a pump	a nozzle	to squeeze	to drive	self-service
a hose	a handle	to choose	to open	

Operation

1. Drive to the gas pumps.
2. Choose a pump so that the gas tank of your car is on the same side as the hose.
3. Get out of the car.
4. Open your gas tank.
5. Choose the kind of gas that you want.
6. Put the nozzle into the gas tank.
7. Turn on the pump.
8. Squeeze the handle on the hose.

Grammar notes

compound nouns — *gas pumps, gas tank*
locative phrases — *on the same side, on the hose*
directional phrase — *drive **to the pumps***
phrasal verbs — *turn on, get out of*
that clause and *so that* clause

Follow-up

1. Do this operation as a pantomime, pretending that students' desks are cars. Using the blackboard or poster paper, the teacher or students can draw gas pumps with different grades of gasoline.

2. Write an amusing story (a paragraph) about trying to get gas at a self-service gas station. The story can be real or imaginary.

3. Write a dialogue or operation for a full-service gas station.

54. Using a Laundromat

Materials   none (This operation can be done as a pantomime.)

Key words

temperature	a load	to take	to put
a laundromat	a washing	to select	to close
a lid	machine	to open	

Operation

1. Take your clothes to the laundromat.
2. Open the lid of a washing machine.
3. Put your clothes into the machine.
4. Select the water temperature and load size.
5. Put in the soap.
6. Close the lid.
7. Put the correct amount of money into the machine.

Grammar notes

possession — *your, of a washing machine*
directional phrases — *take to, put . . . into,*
shift from *a* to *the*

Follow-up

1. Go to a laundromat. Read the directions on the washing machine. Using those directions, write an operation about that specific washing machine. Use specific amounts such as the amount of money and the amount of soap.

2. Go to a laundromat. Watch the people who are there. Take notes on what you see. When you get home, write a paragraph describing the laundromat.

55. Withdrawing Cash with an ATM Card

Materials   none (This operation can be done as a pantomime.)

Key words

identification	a card	to select	to read	to withdraw
a receipt	a slot	to punch in	to put	to remove
a withdrawal	to enter	to press	to take	personal

Operation
1. Read the directions.
2. Put your card into the slot.
3. Punch in your personal identification number (PIN).
4. When the choices appear, select "withdrawal from checking."
5. Enter the amount that you want to withdraw.
6. When your money appears, remove it.
7. When the machine asks if you are finished, press "Yes."
8. Take your receipt.
9. Take your card.

Grammar notes

directional phrase — *into the slot*
possessive adjective — *your*
when clause
want + infinitive
if clause
that clause
compound noun — *identification number*

Follow-up

1. Go to an ATM bank machine with someone who has an ATM bank card. Draw a picture of the machine. When someone puts the card in the machine, what does the machine say? Write down everything the person does and everything the machine says until the process is completed. When you get home, write a complete operation, using all of the details you have written down, on withdrawing cash with an ATM card.

2. Write out the steps for another transaction, such as depositing to a savings account.

Croesus National Bank
MEMBER FDIC

MONEY $ CENTER

580 143 000 0039936

ROBERT A TAFT

BOOSTERVILLE, OHIO 43227

NBS

Robert A. Taft

AUTHORIZED SIGNATURE

This is not a charge card and the depositor agrees that use of this card is subject to all applicable bank rules and regulations and the terms of the account agreements.

MIDWEST 66®

MINUS System®

Verb Index*

*Numbers indicate operation number

Grammar Notes Index*

*Numbers indicate operation number

Supplementary Materials Handbooks

Index Card Games for ESL ◆ **Index Card Games for French** ◆ **Index Card Games for Spanish.** The 6 card games explained in each of these handbooks are easy to prepare and play using 3x5 index cards. These are student-centered, group activities that provide practice with vocabulary, structure, spelling, questioning, and conversation. Sample games are given in the target language.

Families. 10 card games for language learners. 40 colorful playing cards are included.

Conversation Inspirations for ESL. Over 1,200 conversation topics and 6 distinctive conversation activities.

Cue Cards: Nations of the World. Information cards on the 42 most populous nations provide stimulus for 10 communicative activities.

Cue Cards: Famous Women of the 20th Century. Information cards on 40 of the most interesting and influential people of the century provide stimulus for 10 different communicative activities.

Story Cards: The Tales of Nasreddin Hodja. Pair work conversation activities. 40 folk tales for building narrative skills, communicative competence, and fluency, each on a separate illustrated card.

More Index Card Games and Activities for ESL. 9 pair and small-group activities based on the use of 3x5 index cards. Step-by-step explanations of the games are followed by sample materials at different levels of difficulty.

Vocabulary Materials

Lexicarry. An illustrated vocabulary builder for second languages.

Lexicarry Posters. 25 wall charts to facilitate classroom discussion of the vocabulary and of cultural questions suggested by the drawings.

54 Function Flashcards from Lexicarry. Easy-to-handle miniposters illustrate 57 situations requiring functional language. Working together as a class or in pairs, your students will discover hundreds of critically important expressions.

Getting a Fix on Vocabulary. Using words in the news. A vocabulary builder focused on the system of compounding and affixation in English, with exercises and words in the context of news articles.

***Also* The ESL Miscellany.** A cultural and linguistic inventory of American English.

For further information or to order, please write to

Pro Lingua Associates, 15 Elm St., Brattleboro, Vermont 05301
We accept VISA and MASTERCARD orders by phone: 800-366-4775.